THE 9 LIVES OF TYO

THE 9 LIVES OF TYO

A Tale For The Child Within Us All.

Murry Hope

Thoth Publications

Published in the U.K. by Thoth Publications,
c/o BM Sothis, London, WC1N 3XX.

Copyright © 1990 Murry Hope

Cover and artwork by Jana Reichl-Cunningham

ISBN 1 870450 12 4

Printed in Great Britain

MURRY HOPE Author, Lecturer and Founder of
THE INSTITUTE OF TRANSPERSONAL SENSITIVITY

Published Books:
The Way of Cartouche - Oracle of Ancient Egyptian Magic
Practical Techniques of Psychic Self-Defence
Ancient Egypt: The Sirius Connection
The Psychology of Healing
The Psychology of Ritual
The Book of Talimantras
Practical Egyptian Magic
Practical Celtic Magic
Practical Greek Magic
The Greek Tradition
The 9 Lives of Tyo
The Lion People

Books in Progress:
Atlantis: Myth or Reality? (Spring 1991)
Essential Woman: Her Mystery, Her Power. (Spring 1991)
OLYMPUS: An Experience in Self Discovery (Summer 1991)
Time: The Ultimate Energy (Summer 1991)
The Magic of Atlantis (1992)

Recorded Lectures:
Hypnotherapy and Regression
Celtic Magic and The Druids
Mysticism in the Modern World
The Nature and Power of Dreams
Reincarnation, Karma and Heredity
The Healing Power and Magic of Trees
Animals - Do They Have a Psychic Power?
The Kingdoms of Faery, Devas, Elementals and Angels

CONTENTS

To Bast, whom I am honoured to serve.

Tyo, the Crystal People, and his friends Perywin and Gilly...

Introduction

THE PLANET OF THE PASCHATS

If you look into the sky on a clear winter's night you will see a very bright, blue-white star twinkling merrily away on its own. But it isn't really alone; it has a companion star which is very, very small and not so bright, and can only be seen through very powerful telescopes. This was not always so, however, for there was a period when the smaller star-sun was much larger and shone with a golden light, just like our own sun. How it came to shrink, and what happened in that solar system as a result, is all part of another story that I might tell you someday. But for the present my tale concerns the two star-suns as they *used to be*, and two planets that regularly orbited them, one slightly smaller than Earth and the other a little larger.

Long, long ago, when our own solar system was in its infancy, on the smaller of these two planets there lived a race of beings who were not like you and me. They were of the feline species, which means they looked more like our cats, lions or tigers, except that they walked upright on two legs, like we do. They were called Paschats, which means "Cat People". As well as being clever and very wise, they were gentle and kind, and soon made good friends with their planetary neighbours.

The days and nights on the smaller planet were not short like ours; they lasted for long periods. During this time it was cold and very dark indeed, and everyone stayed home and rested. Then would come the medium-light days when the rays of the golden star-sun lit up the little planet for a while, and finally the very bright days would come when the big, blue star-sun smiled happily upon it. It could be very warm then, especially in the places where the crystals grew. But this was as it should be, as the crystals were fed by the big star-sun's energy and supplied the power that met the needs of the people during the dark periods.

1

Now the larger planet was called Ishna, and the people who lived there were known as the Crystal People. They were quite different from the Paschats and more like we are on Earth, except that they were smaller, slighter and very fair, and their bodies had a crystalline look about them. Beautiful crystals grew in their world which they used for many wonderful things - like storing energy and space travel, knowledge which they passed on to the Paschats. Their scholars were particularly good at things like mathematics and astronomy, but they were not a physically strong people, whereas the Paschats were very powerfully built and also quite practical, so the two races together made a good team. In fact, the Crystal People had told them that they were about the strongest race they had met in the many galaxies to which they had travelled.

Paschats had a very strict but happy way of living. Young Paschats always looked after the older ones, for with age went wisdom and grandparents, in particular, were treated with great reverence. There was lots of free time for the young ones to enjoy themselves, but there was also much to be learned. You see, it was not just their own planet and Ishna that they studied at school, but also the many other places that their Elders and the Crystal People had visited during their journeys through space and time.

Both the Paschats and Crystal People knew lots of things that we haven't yet discovered, as their science was a long way ahead of ours. For example, they had learned how to use time warps to travel to other galaxies, and their studies had also taught them that on some distant planets there were animals, birds and plants who were not as happy and well cared for as the creatures in their own worlds. This made them very sad and they were most anxious to understand and help both their own kind and others who were not so fortunate. But the Old Ones who created the many universes also made certain rules, one of which was that one must never interfere with life on other planets. However, there are always special situations that call for an exception to every rule, which is what this story is all about.

In Paschatland there lived a young boy-lion, or cub as we call them, whose name was Tyo. He was a twin, just as all Paschats and Crystal People were, which had something to do with there being two suns, and his sister was called Taku. Like other young felines, Tyo and Taku had learned at school all about other worlds and the creatures that lived in them, so while they were still quite young they decided that when they grew up they would like to be cosmic historians, which means that they would study the minds and customs of all those beings that their Elders and the Crystal People had discovered during their travels through the universe.

In Tyo's world there were no wild animals; all was gentle and well ordered, and everyone respected, loved and understood every other living thing. This meant that the birds, trees, plants and fairy folk were all able to talk to each other, which was both very interesting for everyone and a lot of fun. Plants did not stay fixed in the ground like they do here on Earth; they could pull up their own roots and move around, which was why every Paschat home had a special room that had beds of soft green earth (green being the colour of the soil in Paschatland) where a passing plant could put up for the night, or even stay longer if it so wished. It was the custom that when a plant accepted the hospitality of a Paschat home it would always leave an offering of its fruit, leaves or seeds, and as these visits were frequent, nobody ever went hungry. Of course, Paschats never killed plants by pulling them out of the ground to eat because there was no need to. You see, some of the plants preferred to live together in big communities either in the open or among the trees, so all a Paschat had to do was to pay them a visit and he or she would be given all the food they needed and more.

Paschats did not think of pets in the same way as we do, but rather as friends and equals. Tyo had a plant friend called Gilly. Sometimes he would take Gilly into his own special room where he had a nice tray of green soil, and Gilly would stay with him for the Long Sleep. In addition to his family, Gilly, and his feline friends, Tyo was also very fond of Perywin, the big blue hen who regularly laid the delicious green eggs of which Tyo was particularly fond. But nobody actually ate each other in that land and, apart from the eggs of the blue fowl and those that the water serpents kindly gave them, Tyo, like all other Paschats, lived on the gifts of fruits, nuts, berries and vegetables of all kinds that he and his family either received or collected from the friendly trees and plants.

You may well wonder what Tyo and his family looked like, and whether they wore clothes like we do. Try to imagine a lion standing up on its hind legs and that will give you some idea. Although Paschats had become shorter over the long generations when they had learned to stand erect, they were still a little taller than most humans. Tyo's face was much smaller than that of an African lion and his features more refined. His fine thick mane, of which he was very proud, was a pale golden colour and neatly brushed, just as people here care for and fashion their hair. His ears were more pointed than those of our lions, however, and more like a lynx's.

Paschats came in several colours. There were brown Paschats, golden coloured ones like Tyo, white ones, and mixed ones who sometimes had brown bodies, pale manes and striped legs. Oh yes, of course, they had tails!

Female Paschats, like our lionesses, did not have manes. Their ears were much larger, however, and if you would like to see what a Paschat really was like you should visit the Egyptian Room in any large museum and look at the statues of Sekhmet and Bast. The ancient Egyptians knew all about Paschats because in the very early days of their civilization some had actually met them, while others had heard of them and the Crystal People from the Atlanteans, but that is part of the next chapter as you will see.

What did they wear? Well, although their coats were not as thick as those of some creatures on Earth, they were still quite furry by our standards, so they did not need lots of clothes. But they liked bright colours and their simple garments, which were a little like those worn by the ancient Greeks, were very colourful indeed and often covered with pretty stones and pieces of shining metal. They were also very partial to belts and buckles and it was the custom for everyone to have his or her own special buckle, which was usually made magically by the Paschat metalsmiths living in the mountain caves who, legend had it, had been taught their arts by the Old Ones themselves!

Because all the different creatures could talk mind-to-mind (we call it telepathy), it did not matter whether they spoke each other's language or not, since words were not necessary. Nor did the Paschats think that they were the wisest beings on their planet; in fact, there was an ancient tree named Timbal living in one of the dense forests who was believed to be wiser than anyone else in Paschatland. All the Elders of Tyo's race, including his own mother and father, went to consult Timbal whenever they were in doubt about something. But Timbal was very, very old and

4

inclined to sleep for long periods, so everyone had to wait until he woke up before they could talk to him about their questions and anxieties. Because there were no wars, sickness or cruelty most of the problems that arose were either about personal matters, the weather (which could be very troublesome at times because of the orbits of the two star-suns) or the search for knowledge about other places in the universe, because Paschats were, like all cats, very curious.

Now Tyo's father was a very wise Paschat who had travelled in a spaceship with other Elders of his Pride to visit the Crystal People. When he returned from his journey he told his children about the wonderful double pyramid crystals they had, which you could look into and see what was going on in both the past and present in other parts of the universe. You see, both the Paschats and Crystal People understood all about time, and how to move backwards and forwards through what they called "cosmic time-zones". There was one story which really made Tyo and his sister cry, and that was about a beautiful blue planet far, far away, where felines didn't stand up straight, but walked on all four legs.

"It is a sad, sad state for our people there," Tyo's and Taku's father said to them. "Some of them are large and very wild and no-one has understood them since before the Blue Planet had its great Flood; other felines are gentle and much smaller, but they are treated as possessions, and not as equals at all. In fact, even the humans who rule the planet do not seem to know about the life force that is in all living things."

"But why can't we travel through time to this planet and teach them?" Tyo asked.

"Because, my son, you have many things to learn first. There are rules which must not be broken, and it may not be the will of the Old Ones that we should interfere just yet, or even at all!"

"But there must be *some* way!" Tyo pleaded.

"In time, Timbal will tell you what you should do, but meanwhile you must learn as much as you can about the ways of other worlds, for they are not all as kind and caring as ours." Tyo, being a sensible little lion, was forced to agree.

Tyo and his sister grew to be strong and wise, and when they were older each took a mate in the same way that people here get married and raise families. Tyo's wife was called Shana and she was what we would

5

call a doctor (although Paschat medicine was very different from what we have on Earth) and Shana made a special study of the way *all* creatures think and feel — because they do, you know! And this not only included her own species, but also the plants, birds, trees, other animals, and even their planet itself to which the Crystal People had given the name *Khi-tsa-etu,* "the place of the cats". In fact, Paschats had always known that planets and star-suns were living beings with minds and feelings of their own.

In time, Tyo and Shana had twin cubs and life passed slowly and happily for them all. One day when Tyo was quite old by Paschat sun-years, Timbal sent a message for him to come and visit. Tyo made his way to the depth of the forest where Timbal lived and approached the Wise One.

"What have you to tell me now that I am growing old, for I will soon shed this tired pelt for a new one?" Tyo asked.

"You have worked hard and learned much, Tyo," Timbal replied, "and, in view of what you have always wanted to do since you were a cub, the Old Ones have decided that you are now ready to go to the Blue Planet that orbits the single yellow sun. On that planet there is much sadness, which you will be able to learn about and record to bring back to your ancestors when you finally return to them in many light-years' time." Timbal and the Paschats knew that all time is really one, which is a secret that the people on the Blue Planet had not yet discovered.

"You will not be permitted to time-travel there and appear as a Paschat for two good reasons: Firstly, it would give you an unfair advantage over the creatures that live there; and, secondly, you would most certainly frighten them, especially the humans who would attack you and try to drive you away. Besides, how can you learn to feel and suffer as they do unless you are born amongst them in a form familiar to them? This will mean, of course, that you will grow up there knowing things that they do not, but you will not be able to tell anyone. Apart from a very few who will be aliens like yourself, most of the natives have not yet learned to use their minds to talk to other species. In time, however, after their planet has had two changes in its axis, they will develop that gift, but for now, proud feline, remember what I have told you. When you arrive there be prepared to see and experience things that your race has either never known or long since forgotten."

"What sort of things, please, Timbal?" Tyo asked the old tree.

"Tears, pain, suffering, hatred, rejection; but also caring, warmth and most of all *LOVE*. But never fear; you will not be alone there for Taku and Shana have chosen to go with you. And your father, who shed his pelt four sun-cycles ago, is also waiting to join you. You will also meet a few of the Crystal People on the Blue Planet. But a word of advice: Do not expect everyone to look as they do now, for they will not be wearing the bodies that you are used to, just as you yourself will have to bend and walk on all fours once again as your people did in times long past.

"While you are there, Tyo, you will always be born into a feline form. But, because the humans on the Blue Planet do not speak our mind language, your sister Taku has agreed to be as one of them. Now it is only on very rare occasions that the Old Ones allow this to happen, as it is particularly difficult for a feline to adjust to a human body. The two species are so different it will be uncomfortable and frustrating for Taku at times, but she is strong in mind and spirit and is willing to take on the challenge. Together you will be able to give help, comfort and love to many."

Before Tyo could ask any more of the questions that were spinning through his head Timbal continued.

"No, I will not tell you any more, but go with my blessing and that of the Old Ones. Never lose faith in who and what you are! And remember, true Cosmic Love is the greatest force in the universe!" With that the old tree bowed its massive head and slipped peacefully into one of its long, long sleeps. And that was how Tyo first came to know that he would be going to the Blue Planet that we call Earth.

In time, Tyo, Taku and Shana each shed their old furry bodies and joined their ancestors in the realms of the Old Ones to rest with their kin before taking on their big tasks. Paschats, like Crystal People, had always known that bodies were only something one wore for a little while in order to look in on and learn from different cosmic time-zones.

7

Tyo loved her mother's beautiful collar…

Life No. 1:

ATLANTIS

The sun's rays were streaming through the tall pillars of the great white Temple as Kalon, the High Priest, made his way to the lion gardens where Tula, his favourite lioness, was about to give birth to a cub. Kalon knew the exact hour when the cub would be born, for he had worked it all out from the stars. He also knew that this cub would be a rather special little person, but then Kalon was a very wise High Priest, which was as things ought to be.

Tula and her mate, Rhe-ien, lived in a beautiful park beside the vast Temple. Every day they took a walk with Kalon, one of the humans mentioned by Timbal who, because he had once lived on the Crystal Planet, could understand the language of all creatures. But, of course, in those days before the Great Flood a lot of the humans were much closer and kinder to nature than they are today.

As Kalon entered the enclosure where Tula was resting he knew her time was near, so he asked the young novice priest who looked after the lions to take Rhe-ien to another part of the enclosure, for he knew the great beast might be distressed if he heard his mate cry out. But Tula made no sound when her cub was born, and after she had washed her baby she allowed Kalon and Rhe-ien to take a look — but only a quick one, as her low growl soon told them when it was time to leave her and her little one to rest.

Kalon sat down quietly with his wife, Danu, who was a beautiful priestess, and together they talked mind to mind to Rhe-ien about what they should call the new little lioness.

"She must have brought a name with her from her native planet," said Danu, who knew about such things.

9

"Then who better to tell us than Rhe-ien, who must surely have come from the same place," Kalon exclaimed.

So they asked Rhe-ien, who thought long and hard before responding, "Her name is Tyo!"

"Is that a male or female name?" Danu asked.

"Does it really matter?" Rhe-ien replied. "After all, if it was very personal to her on the Paschat planet, surely it can be used either way here as it is not a name that anyone else has." They all agreed, so Tyo she was named.

At first Tyo found it very strange running around on all fours, although, of course, she didn't quite know why, but she soon got used to it. "When you are older," Tula told her, "you will receive a beautiful present from Kalon, just as your father and I have." She rubbed her strong neck against the silver collar that she wore around it. It was bright and shiny and studded with blue stones that sparkled in the sunlight, and it reminded Tyo of something that she couldn't quite remember. Tyo loved her mother's collar, for to her it was a living thing. At night, before she went to sleep, Tyo would talk to the blue stones and ask them how long it would be before she could have a friend like Kalon all to herself. One day Tyo's parents decided she was old enough to meet more of Kalon's people.

"We could not take you with us before," her father told her, "for young lionesses must pay heed to what they are told and not make loud noises when everyone else is quiet. Also, they must learn that if they are to have a human friend like Kalon they must return love for love, and service for service. If you work with a priest or priestess, you will be loved, fed, and kept well in mind and body. You, in turn, must learn to read his or her mind and know what certain sounds mean. You must also drive away anything, visible or invisible, that might cause harm to those who care for you. In time you will sit at the Judgment Seat, but such things are for the priests to teach you as you grow up."

Rhe-ien swished his great mane with an air of distinction and Tyo thought to herself how lucky she was to have such a beautiful and wise father. Of course, she had not the slightest idea what he was talking about but, as we shall see, she was soon to learn.

Rhe-ien did not wear a collar like Tula, but he had a solid gold band around his left leg, with his own name and Kalon's engraved upon it.

The days were happy ones for a baby lioness. Once a week her father and mother would go to the great white Temple to sit by the Judgment Seat with Kalon and help him to make the right decisions about the people who came there for a hearing. This is because felines can see things that humans do not see and, although they may not speak our language, they have their own ways of making their message known, as we shall shortly see.

One day Tyo's father told her that it was time for her to be taken to the big Temple to watch them make judgments together. "You must also learn how to do this, my daughter," said Rhe-ien. "Although you are still only a little lioness, you have brought a lot of wisdom over with you from Paschatland, but it needs to be trained for Temple service on this planet." Tyo was quite excited about this, of course, although she had to confess that she was also a little nervous. After all, it was a very BIG Temple!

It was quite early in the morning and the day was obviously going to be a hot one. A faint mist rose from the many canals of the capital as the three lions set out with Kalon and his family towards the great Temple where the judgments were to be heard. Kalon went first across the blue tiled courtyard, up the long flight of white steps that glistened in the clear, early sunlight, through the marbled lobby and down the centre aisle towards the Chair of Judgment, which stood on a huge, shining dias. Danu followed behind him with their young son, whose name was Helio, and finally came the three lions — one large, stately and magnificent, one sleek, shiny and beautiful, and one small, downy and clumsy.

Tyo made her way towards the spot that her father indicated, trying very hard to be as quiet as possible, but the claws on her little paws seemed to make such loud noises on the floor and when she tried to "make velvet" as she had been taught, she kept skidding on the polished marble! In spite of all her efforts to be as silent as possible she found herself letting out a monstrously loud "purrrr" which seemed to amuse Helio, who started to giggle.

After they had all settled down one of the attendants brought in the first case. It was a rather strange looking man, dirty and unkempt. He was clutching something in his hands that sparkled, and which he held onto very tightly as though he were afraid that someone would take it away from him. There was a look of fear in his eyes and Tyo didn't like his scent at all. In fact, she growled quietly to herself, but her mother nipped her gently so that she should not give Kalon the wrong impression. This puzzled the little lioness, for she didn't think the man was at all nice. Kalon asked the Scribe to read the charge.

"This man," he read, "who cannot remember his name, has stolen this bracelet from an honest woman's dwelling and he will not return it. He says that it is his, but the woman has proof that it is her property."

"Why do you wish to own this trinket?" Kalon asked the man, who trembled and fondled the bracelet before answering.

"It is the colour, my lord, it takes the pain from my head!"

"That I can well understand," Kalon replied, "you are indeed sick and in need of the silver ray to bring you relief. Come, give it back to the lady and I will give you something to take its place."

He beckoned to a young priestess in a green robe standing nearby, who presented him with a tray that was laden with many sparkling objects. Kalon selected a bright silver chain which he handed to the man.

"You must wear this while our healers attend to your sickness and make you well again."

The man fell upon his knees and clasped the chain gratefully to his breast. "Thank you, my lord," he whispered gratefully. Tyo saw a big tear splash on the shiny floor where he knelt and she was so sorry that she had growled when she shouldn't have.

"So shall it be according to the wisdom and understanding of the Old Ones," answered Kalon. As he spoke he raised his hands and made a sign over the man who was then escorted away by a gentle healer-priestess. As Kalon made the sign Tyo noticed a stream of silver light leave his hands and enter the man. Once again, Tyo half remembered something, but she wasn't quite sure what.

Rhe-ien then explained to his daughter. "When people come for judgment do not look at them on the outside only, or pay too much heed to the smells or sounds that come from them, but look rather at the aura around them."

"What is an aura?" Tyo enquired.

"It is a light that surrounds all living things," said Rhe-ien. "As

12

everything is alive, that means that everything has an aura. Auras come in many colours, shapes and sizes, and when they are bright and clear that is good. But anyone who has an aura which is dark, or cloudy, or broken may well make strange noises, smell badly, or not look quite right. This means that they are sick and should be helped by the healer-priests, so you must not growl at such persons, my daughter."

Tyo wanted very much to see an aura so she stole a quick glance at Kalon. She wasn't too sure whether she was imagining things so she looked again, this time much harder and, sure enough, there was a beautiful blue light edged with gold all around him. Of course, after that she simply had to take another "hard" look — this time at the priestess, whose aura was a sort of silvery crystal colour. And then Tyo understood.

After that, Kalon asked Tyo to sit at the back for a while and watch how her parents worked with him while he heard the next few cases, so there she sat very quietly and very patiently, watching everything that went on, and trying very hard to take in as much as she could. But when it came to the last case of the day Tyo had the surprise of her life when Kalon beckoned her to come forward.

"Now it is your turn to let us see what you have learned, little one," said the kindly High Priest.

Tyo tried to look as important as she could, which meant sitting up very straight like her parents did. But somehow it didn't quite work out, for she got an itch on her tummy and kept falling over each time she tried to scratch it, although no-one seemed to worry so neither did she.

The first man to enter did not look at all bad. He was dressed nicely, and seemed to do all the right things like giving the lions a friendly smile and bowing most humbly before Kalon. He was followed close behind by a very young priest who obviously hadn't been in office very long and who seemed rather unsure of himself.

Kalon asked for an account of the case and the Scribe read as follows: "This young priest, whose name is Indris, was left in charge of the Temple in the small town of Khar-kris while his superior was away at the capital attending to matters of State. Indris claims that during this period he caught Tallus, the merchant, who stands before us, trying to steal secrets which are allowed only to those of high office, from the chamber of the Senior Priest. These he thought to make use of to gain power over his fellowmen."

"Come, Indris," Kalon addressed the young priest, "and tell us of these things."

The young man seemed very shy and his voice was unsteady. Tyo found herself feeling a little suspicious until she suddenly noticed her mother leaning towards him with love and warmth glistening in her fine eyes. Indris spoke very softly.

"My lord, it was late in the evening and I noticed a light from within the Temple offices. I entered, and found this man, Tallus, in the private chamber of my superior, copying from a large book, the sight of which is forbidden to all but those of our Order. I told him that what he was doing was wrong and he replied that if I would say nothing of this to anyone and forget the matter he would shower me with many gifts. Naturally, I refused. Then he insisted that he himself should have been a priest and therefore the knowledge was rightly his, but due to a misjudgment he was never accepted for the priestly office. When I made my path of duty quite clear to him he threatened me with evil words, saying I was sick in my mind and had imagined what I had seen. Many people in our city believe his words and feel that I have wronged a good man and am therefore unworthy of my calling."

"And you, Tallus, how do you answer to this?" Kalon asked, addressing the older man. The merchant seemed very confident and sincere in his reply.

"My lord, I approached the Temple that evening to speak with Indris about my daughter, for this young man would court her if I were to permit it. But, because I am not too happy about his character, I have held back my consent and the reason for my visit was to tell him that my word on this matter was final. He said he would not accept this and would blacken my good name with evil lies unless I changed my mind."

"'It is untrue, my lord!" gasped Indris.

But the merchant ignored the interruption and continued. "I am sorry for the boy for he is young and sick, no doubt, so I ask you to judge him kindly and I will forgive and forget."

Tyo was quite puzzled by now. At first she had felt sorry for the young priest and then the older man had seemed so nice, so she turned to her father and mother for help.

Kalon spoke to Indris. "Is it true that you would court the daughter of this merchant?"

Indris hung his head and answered slowly, "Yes, my lord."

There was a pause before Kalon spoke again. "Then stand forth, priest." He indicated a spot in front of him. "And do you still hold that your story is the truth?"

Poor Indris looked as if all was lost as he whispered, "Yes, my lord."

Kalon then made a sign to Tyo's parents and they both slowly rose, stretched themselves to their full height and approached the young priest with a stealthy grace. Indris stood firm. They circled him widely at first and then closed in, until Rhe-ien's huge mane was brushing against the blue sash of his robe. Suddenly Tyo's mother sat down with a plop, right at Indris' feet and licked his bare toes, purring loudly. There was a moments' pause, then Kalon beckoned Indris to stand down and motioned the two great beasts to return to their places. He then asked Tallus to come forward and stand where Indris had stood, and Tyo suddenly realized that the High Priest was calling HER!

"Come forth, my little one, and let us see what you have learned today." Tyo's fluffy little legs seemed to shake under her as she made her way towards the tall figure of the merchant who looked so grand in his fine clothes and sparkling jewels. In fact, he spoke to the little lioness in a soft, kindly voice.

"Hello, little girl," said Tallus, "let us be friends. Come, lick my hand."

Tyo felt much braver after that. She was just about to give him a lick when she thought she noticed a slight movement behind him which startled her. Was she imagining it, or was there something there? She took a hard look at his aura, the same as she had done with Kalon and his lady, and although it was not a pretty colour it appeared clear enough. And yet it seemed to Tyo that things weren't quite as they should be. She shivered and growled, not at Tallus himself but at something behind him. She circled round him in the way her parents had shown her and there it was — a small, sinister ball of evil energy! She took a deep breath and, half in anger and half in fear, let out the loudest roar her little lungs could muster and Tallus nearly jumped out of his skin! It was only the firm grip of her father's teeth on her small tail that prevented her from leaping at the dark intruder that only she, her family, and Kalon and Danu could see.

Kalon's soothing voice spoke kindly in her ears. "Well done, little one, you have inherited both your parents' sight and wisdom. From now on you will come to the Temple regularly for training at the Seat of Judgment."

Kalon's judgment was, of course, in favour of Indris. Tallus was sent to the priests to be exorcised, which means that they would take away the nasty dark thing that Tyo had seen, and then give him healing and help. Kalon had also found out that Tallus' daughter was very fond of Indris, so they were allowed to pursue their love with the blessing of the High Priest.

What a trying morning for a small lioness! Poor Tyo was quite exhausted, and as she walked beside her parents towards the big Temple doors her little legs felt weak. So weak, in fact, that she didn't jump when a silvery young voice spoke in her ear.

"Hello, little woolly one."

She turned and looked into the freckled face of young Helio. It was a friendly face, full of fun and frolic but also warm and caring. Tyo liked what she saw so she put her tongue out as far as it would go and gave the upturned nose a VERY wet lick.

"Oh, fie, you messy cub," gurgled Helio. "If you and I are to be friends then it must be two-sided." And so saying he threw his arms around the little lioness' neck and the two of them toppled bumpety-bump down the Temple's white steps.

And that was the start of a friendship that was to survive not only the sun drenched days of Atlantis, but colder, more cruel times when the justice of lions and humans would become confused in the dark mists of time. For Helio was none other than his sister Taku who had taken on her first human body, just as Timbal had foretold.

16

When the Old Ones created all things it was their wish that there should be harmony, love and understanding among all living creatures. But there are unfriendly forces around the Blue Planet that do not want it to be that way, which is why things are as they are down here.

There were also statues of Paschats...

LIFE No. 2

ANCIENT EGYPT

Tyo had learned many things during his life in Atlantis, one of which was that people just did not think in the same way that lions did. He had also learned that lions were not the only felines on the Blue Planet and, if he was to be of any help there at all, he must live in those branches of the cat family that would bring him closer to humans and other creatures. His Atlantean days as a lioness had seen him in the company of his sister, Taku, a father and mother who were also Paschats, and Kalon and Danu who were Crystal People. So in a way it had been a sheltered life, but it had given him the chance to get used to the way things are on Earth.

Helio eventually succeeded Kalon as High Priest and Tyo served him well, but in the fullness of time they both returned to their ancestors for a rest. During that period many changes had taken place on the Blue Planet. The rains of the Great Flood had come and gone and the great Temple now lay at the bottom of the sea. Tyo knew the time was right for him to return to Earth to learn some more, but he wasn't quite sure where he ought to go. So he thought of what Timbal might suggest, and with that he drifted into a nice, calm sleep.

The sun shone fiercely outside, but inside the Temple walls everything was cool and dark as the brown queen cat gave birth to her three kittens: a striped male and two brown females with silvery tips on their fur. Tyo cuddled close to his mother as he knew that this time he was no longer a lioness, but a sturdy little tom kitten. The mother cat, who was broad and soft, cuffed her son.

"You are a greedy one and no mistake," she scolded. "Stay back and let your sisters feed."

Tyo sniffed each of them, but only one responded. He sent her the thought, "Have you been on this planet before?"

"Yes," the thought came back to him.

"Where and when?" Tyo asked.

"I was a white *chata* in the Old Country," his sister replied. Of course by the Old Country she meant Atlantis, which Tyo knew because all small cats were called *chatas* in that land.

Whether or not their mother picked up these thoughts she never said, so neither of her bright kittens knew whether she was also from the Old Country, although they rather suspected she was not. But she was a kind and good mother, which is what every young kitten needs.

Tyo soon grew big and strong and there were lots of other cats to play with in the Temple compound, but they were never allowed to go outside. Their food was brought to them each day by a young lad who served at the Temple. He was good and kind and, although he didn't smell quite as nice as the Temple people in the Old Country, Tyo was happy when he stroked him and told him what a fine kitten he was.

Many of the cats and kittens wore shiny golden earrings that shone brightly in the light of the Temple lamps. Being sacred animals they were allowed the freedom of the Temple, and Tyo liked nothing better than to wander amongst the tall columns to see what interesting things he could find. In the main hall there was a large, golden statue of a ram. The boy who looked after them said it was a god called "Amon" who sometimes liked to appear that way. There were also statues of Paschats, although the people had long forgotten who they really were and thought they were gods or goddesses.

One morning there was a great deal of fuss and noise. People were running round the Temple in all directions and shouting things to each other, so Tyo asked his mother what had happened.

"The old Pharaoh has died, my son," she meowed.

"What is a Pharaoh, and what does 'died' mean?" Tyo asked curiously.

"The Pharaoh is the king and kings are related to the gods, so they are rather special. 'Died' is what humans call going to sleep forever and never waking up. We all do it in the end, you know." Tyo now knew that dying was the same as shedding one's pelt in Paschatland, so that was another lesson he had learned. But being a curious kitten he continued to ask questions.

"What will happen now, Mother?"

"Nothing very much. There will be a new Pharaoh and everything will go on just as before, once they have got over the fuss of burying this one."

"What's 'burying,' Mother?"

"Goodness me, you are a curious kitten! Well, for most people and that also goes for lots of animals, somebody digs a hole in the ground and in goes the pelt of the one that has died. But when a Pharaoh dies he is buried in a much grander manner! I've never seen it myself, but your father once told me — and he heard it from another cat — that there are very special places, like palaces, that Pharaohs go to when they die, with lots to eat and drink and all sorts of beautiful things. People call these places 'tombs'."

"But if he's gone back to his ancestors, surely he wouldn't need anything to eat!" Tyo reasoned.

"That's enough for now, my son! No more of these silly questions. I don't know all the answers anyway, so I would probably tell you wrongly if I guessed."

Although Tyo's mother was not impressed with the coming of the new Pharaoh, the little kitten himself was far from sure about it all. Something in the tip of his tail told him that strange forces were about, and that a little cat might see even stranger sights if he kept his ears and eyes alert and his whiskers twitching. And so it was.

The Pharaoh was duly buried, and what a fuss everyone made about it all! His body was wrapped up tightly, so that for a long time he would stay looking like he had when he was alive. Tyo thought this was very silly. After all, why hold on to one's old, worn out pelt when there were plenty of new ones for the taking after one had rested with one's ancestors for a while! Humans certainly appeared to have gone downhill since the times of the Old Country! Tyo couldn't help wondering whether there were any humans around who remembered those times. It wasn't long before he was to have the answer.

Time passed and for a while nothing seemed to happen. Then, one day the new Pharaoh came to visit the Temple. All of the sacred cats were gathered round to greet him, their tails erect and their fur and whiskers well groomed. When he entered Tyo was surprised to see how young he

21

was — why, he was not much older than the boy who brought their food! He looked fondly at the cats and bent to stroke a few of them.

"What fine cats they are," he exclaimed, "but why are they not allowed to play in the sun?"

Now that comment rang a bell. Tyo thought hard and, come to think of it, the Temple did seem awfully dark sometimes. There were other lights outside, bright, friendly lights, that often peeped round the tall pillars into the gloom of the inner chambers.

"Release them to the outer courtyard where they may frolic in the bright rays of the Creator," the Pharaoh said

The attendant priest shuddered. "But these are sacred cats, sire, dedicated to the goddess Bast. Such an act would be sacrilege. Besides, they might escape or be stolen."

"All creatures of the great god Ra-Horakhti have the right to partake of His light if they so wish. Open the doors so that His furry children may walk in more natural surroundings," he ordered.

The priests were still arguing their point with the Pharaoh's officials when the cats were taken to the large outer doors through which they were never normally allowed to pass. The latches were raised and the large portals ground slowly open.

At first Tyo was almost blinded by the light, which was big and white, or was it yellow? To tell the truth he wasn't quite sure. He blinked for a moment and then ducked behind a high pillar where it was darker to give his eyes a moment to adjust. As the humans withdrew, the cats remained, still and silent. Then, slowly, one by one, they walked back into the darker parts of the Temple, content to live where they had always lived and where they felt secure — all except Tyo! His mother was the first to make her views known.

"That man does not seem like a Pharaoh to me. I shall stay here, as my parents did before me and their parents before them. I am well satisfied with *my* quarters. I have no desire to go out into the world!"

The others all seemed to agree, even their elderly uncle who was so old that nobody knew quite how long he had been there. But Tyo liked the feel of the bright, warm light and wanted to know more about what went on in the world outside. His instincts told him that if he left the comfort of the Temple there would be no young attendant to feed him, no clean place to sleep, and perhaps other humans and creatures who would not be his friends. For a long time he sat and thought. The more he thought about it, the more he felt that he should go out into the big world to find out what else there was that lived under the big, bright light they called Ra-Horakhti.

He waited until the other cats were sound asleep, curled up cosily in their high, softly cushioned baskets, and then he crept silently out past the huge doors into the courtyard beyond. The big, bright light seemed to have gone out; perhaps it, too, had to go to sleep sometime and would return later. The space beneath the big outer gates was just enough for a small cat to squeeze under — one good wriggle and Tyo was free.

What a lot of things there were for an inquisitive kitten to see and do in such a big, strange world! There were new scents, new sounds, and a vast city to be explored. But all was quiet now, for the humans, like the Temple cats, were asleep. Tyo roamed around and explored to his heart's content, without anyone to stop him. After what seemed to be a very long time he became quite tired and hungry. The excitement of the day had proven too much for him and he looked for a sheltered place to rest his tired little legs. He squeezed his furry body through a hole in a wall and found himself on a stone shelf. There was a smell of some sort of food around, but by then Tyo was much too tired even to search for it and he soon fell fast asleep. He was awakened by a lot of noise and somebody shouting.

"Husband, come quickly, there is a cat in the pantry."

"Goodness, wife, why do you shout so; now, where is this beast?"

Tyo blinked and his eyes met first a pair of brown eyes which were owned by a rather fat female human, and then a second and even larger pair of eyes set into the wizened face of a small, thin man who wore something wrapped round his head.

"That, Fayida, is a Temple cat! See its earrings!"

"Then cut them off and sell them, you stupid man, no one will know!"

"Woman, you are the stupid one! If we return this cat to the priests we will get more silver than that rascal of a dealer in the market would give me for the earrings."

23

The woman pondered for a moment. "That is true, husband, then let us do it quickly. Fetch a basket and we will take him back to the Temple. Hurry!"

The man picked Tyo up by the scruff of his neck and popped him into a large wicker basket which he then closed and fastened with a rope. Poor Tyo spat and kicked, but to no avail; his freedom was gone and soon it would be back to the old life again. The basket was duly bundled into a donkey cart and off they went, bumpety-bump down the narrow street. One thing that did cheer Tyo was the fact that the sun had obviously awakened from its sleep, for its beams stole slyly through the slits in the basket.

They hadn't travelled very far, however, when Tyo heard a loud commotion. A riot had started and people seemed to be throwing things at each other and screaming. Inside the basket poor Tyo was quite frightened. What *could* he do? He heard his captor protest as somebody pulled him down from the driving seat of the cart, and the donkey brayed loudly as it bolted and ran away, taking with it the cart and its precious cargo. Tyo's little body ached as he was thrown from side to side. Suddenly he felt the basket pitch forward and then all was blackness.

"He's coming round now," a voice was saying. It was a nice, kind, female voice and it reminded Tyo of the lady priestesses in the Old Country. Tyo tried to move his paws, but one of them did not seem to work properly. He leaned forward and sniffed it to see what was wrong and hit his nose on something hard, which smelled like wood.

"You broke your little leg and we have mended it for you. Soon it will heal and you will be able to run around again."

Tyo looked up at the owner of the voice. She was young and pretty and wore a beautiful green robe. Behind her was a large square opening in the wall through which the lovely, warm sunlight streamed. Although his leg hurt, Tyo was happy. He loved the warm, bright light and he liked the young girl in the green gown. The girl spoke again.

"You see, it was all our fault! My brother had the idea to visit the market end of the city and see what it was like down there. The priests did warn us not to go and said it would start trouble. It's a dirty old city, anyway. My brother says when he's older he will build a fine, new city in the south where the streets are broader and all the children of Ra-Horakhti may travel safely in peace and love."

24

She lifted Tyo gently out of the basket where he had been lying and rubbed him lovingly under the chin. He mewed and purred his thanks. There was a sound and the girl in green turned round.

"Ah, Nefer-kheperu-ra," she said, "here is the poor creature we rescued from the street. He is bruised and has an injured leg, but otherwise he is none the worse for the experience."

The figure that approached was a familiar one; he looked Tyo in the face and gently fingered a striped ear. "This, sister, is one of the sacred Temple cats I saw yesterday. He must have escaped when they opened the outer doors. It is an omen from the gods, so we must see that he is well kept. I will appoint one of my own priests to care for him. Ask one of the servants to summon Meryra."

"It shall be done," said the girl in green, as she put Tyo down gently on a fine, fat cushion. She returned very soon with a young man. His skin was fairer than any of the other people Tyo had seen and his eyes were blue. The Pharaoh addressed him.

"Meryra, take this kitten and care for him; he has suffered on our account because we did not heed wise words. Come, the hour is noon and we must pay our respects to the Great One. Bring him along, too."

Meryra lifted Tyo, cushion and all, and together they made their way from the bright room down a long passage at the end of which there was another room. As Tyo looked up he noticed that there was a big hole in the ceiling through which the white light shone happily down on them all. Meryra placed Tyo on the floor beside him and the humans all knelt silently, as if they were waiting for something special to happen. And soon it did!

Tyo's eyes followed their glances. On the wall in front of them was a large disk of gold from which the sun's rays stretched forth like kindly hands, one of which held a symbol that Tyo definitely recognized as being from the Old Country — the ankh, or Key of Life. As the sun's bright light struck the golden disk it shimmered and seemed to come alive. Then the Pharoah spoke:

"Great Ra-Horakhti, Father of all Creation, shine upon us all and bestow your great blessings, and in your healing rays consider this small creature who has suffered an injury on our account," he intoned. It was

25

at that moment that Tyo remembered the Old Ones and how to recognize them.

Tyo and Meryra lived happily together for many moons and they would have long conversations together about the Old Country and Paschatland, for Tyo discovered that Meryra was one of the Crystal People that Timbal had told him about. After awhile they all moved to a new palace in the south where things were bright and clean and where Tyo was able to roam freely in the beautiful gardens. But all was not well, and although everyone was kind and loving to him, Tyo felt they were secretly anxious about something rather important.

One day Meryra had visitors. Tyo did not like them from the start; they reminded him of the bad people who used to come for judgment in the Old Country. Tyo could see strange shadows around their bodies, which he knew were not as they should be. He tried to warn Meryra, but being the Pharaoh's personal secretary the young priest insisted that he had to meet with them.

"One cannot shun people because one suspects their intentions, little cat," Meryra said to him. "After all, with kindness and love one may even be able to help them to mend their ways."

But Tyo growled quietly to himself. As he saw it, people were either nice or they were not, and it was his duty to keep the not so nice ones away from those he loved and he kept a constant vigil while the visitors remained.

All was well until the Sun God, to whom the Pharaoh had now given the new name of "Aten", turned his smile to other lands and it became dark. Tyo lay curled up in his basket in the passage outside Meryra's room, from which vantage point he kept guard. For a while all was quiet, then suddenly there was a slight noise and Tyo pricked up his ears. The figure of a man was approaching stealthily from the other end of the passage and he stole past where Tyo lay watching and entered the room where Meryra was sleeping.

Tyo's little heart was beating fast as he crouched low to the ground and followed the figure. From the folds of his robe the man withdrew a hand and Tyo saw the glint of a knife. As it was raised above the sleeping Meryra, Tyo sprang. There was a scream as he buried his teeth and claws in the man's arm, a shout and a scuffle, and then Tyo felt a brief stab of pain. Then, suddenly, he was no longer a Temple cat; he was Tyo, the

Paschat, and he was looking down on a scene of confusion. Armed guards were tying the hands of the stranger and Meryra was weeping over the body of a small, striped cat.

This life had been full of valuable lessons. Tyo had learned the joy of sacrificing his life for one he loved, and he also had experienced the first pangs of sorrow. Silently, he withdrew to the spirits of his ancestors to rest and ponder.

The snake went limp and Tyo rolled free...

Life No. 3:

AMAZONIA

Tyo had been greatly saddened by what he had seen on his last visit to the Blue Planet. There was little or no friendship between men and beasts, humans fought against each other, and many animals were hunted and cruelly treated. In fact, things were no longer anything like they had been in the Old Country. Even his beloved Meryra, who had cared for him while he had been a striped tom cat, had also returned to his ancestors. Tyo could see no familiar faces among the people of Earth so he decided to go and live amongst his own kind for a change, so that he could learn their ways and so understand their sufferings, hopes and fears.

The river was wide, the jungle thick and tangled, and the screech of the birds called to everything that the sun was rising over the swampy banks. The mottled yellow and black female jaguar writhed and she whimpered to herself as her two cubs were born. Her mate patrolled the nearby bank, ever heedful of predators and anxious to ward off unwelcome guests with his low, persistent growls. Tyo's father was big and strong and, although his coat was dark, in the bright sunshine the mottled markings could be seen under his sleek fur.

Only too aware that "he" was once more a "she", Tyo blinked at the green maze around her, as her eyes gradually opened. Below her the river washed past and the water spirits sang sweetly, just like they used to in Paschatland. The sun peeped shyly through the tall trees and in the background there was the chattering of many creatures Tyo had never seen or heard before.

This was a new life. There were no humans around, only animals. Tyo's parents, who were kind and understanding, lost no time in explaining to their two offspring what they needed to learn in order to survive. One of the most important things was always to be on the watch for predators. There were lots of unpleasant animals around, but none more vicious than the large, coiling snake. A clever jaguar could overcome such an enemy, but he or she needed the help of a mate.

Then there was the question of one's dinner. In this strange, humid place there were no kindly priests to serve a cat food on a plate. Only that which was caught and killed was available, and Tyo had never done any hunting before.

Tyo's parents were both very religious and worshipped a goddess whom they called "The Huntress."

"But who is She?" Tyo asked.

"She is the Great Huntress," her father told her. "Sometimes She appears as one of us — sometimes as another animal, and other times as a soft light darting among the trees. She is the Great One who helps creatures like ourselves to survive on this cruel planet.

"Is this really a cruel planet, father, cruel all over?" Tyo asked.

"It is a very bad place," her father continued, "and we of the cat family are obliged to kill other creatures or else we, too, would die."

But surely it was not always so?" Tyo was puzzled.

"No, indeed, there were days in the past..." He stopped, as if such times were too painful to recall.

Tyo cut in, "I, too, know of those days..." But before she could say another word her father spoke firmly.

"Then you must never ever think of them or try to recall them, for such memories will bring you nothing but sadness. It is good that creatures should forget other lives if they were good ones, especially if times are hard. In this way they will best cope with what is happening in the present."

And so Tyo forgot all about the Old Country and settled down to the task of learning to hunt and survive in the jungle. Tyo's family always hunted together. Mother would go on ahead and attract the attention of any unfriendly beast that might be lurking around to pounce on them. Once a creature had shown itself, she would entice it towards her, but always keeping just out of its reach. Then father would come up from behind it and finish it off. Tyo thought that this was a very clever way of doing things, as the attacker usually thought it was only dealing with one cat. On one occasion a large snake attacked their mother, and Tyo and her brother jumped up and down anxiously when their father did not seem to be doing anything about it. But just as the evil grip started to tighten, father's jaws closed on it from behind so suddenly that it could not have known what hit it! Tyo was so excited that in her effort to help she caught the thrashing tail in her teeth and bit it as hard as she could.

Mother and father always hunted for food and when they had made a kill there was a strict order for eating. Tyo and her brother ate first, then father and finally mother. The reason why her parents did not eat at the same time was simple. One always stood guard so that the other could eat in peace. When Tyo and her brother reached maturity they had to join the other end of the queue and have what was left over after their parents had had first pickings. The day eventually came when Tyo's parents called her and her brother together for a serious talk.

"Children, you are no longer youngsters and must now make your way in the jungle alone. Tyo, you must find a mate and rear your own young; and you, my son, must travel afar and seek territory which you can mark as your own. When you have done this you can look for a female to share your land with you, for such is the way of nature. It is therefore right that we should chase you away, lest you become too used to the ease of home life with us where all is done for you."

Tyo knew that these were words of love and therefore she and her brother were not troubled when her parents growled at them and chased them off into the jungle, far beyond the land her father had marked as his domain.

Such times are hard for a young female jaguar. Without a mate to hunt with the chances of survival are slim indeed. Tyo wandered through the dense undergrowth not daring to lie down and rest for fear of enemies. Her parents had taught her to swim, so the swift river torrents did not frighten her. She decided to cross to the other side, but not at the broad part. Further along there were places where the two banks were closer together. It would be easier to cross there.

After trudging many miles in silence Tyo became anxious. How could she hope to find a mate if there were no other jaguars in the area to sense her presence? If she were to call, her enemies would also know her whereabouts. Tyo thought and thought. She was not really afraid of many creatures, only the long snakes that twist and entwine themselves

31

around their victim's body. These evil creatures had squeezed the life out of many a fine cat in the past!

Tyo flopped down exhausted. She could hear the wash of the water just ahead, but she now felt too tired to swim the river. She made her protest in the form of a loud roar which said: "If you are the mate for me and you are out there among those trees, come to me. I am here, and I am tired and hungry." And so saying she dropped off to sleep.

But Tyo had not been asleep very long before a strange sense of danger caused her to wake up. She opened first one eye, then the other. There was a rustle in the nearby grass and Tyo saw before her the thickest and longest snake she had ever seen in her life — much longer, in fact, than the one her father had killed for her mother! She froze with fear and dared not move.

Slowly her wits returned to her. From the sound of the water she knew she could not be more than a short distance from the river, perhaps only a few feet. If only she could tackle this monster in the open... Inch by inch she started to edge away, but the snake followed stealthily, gaining on her with its every movement. As her retreating paws touched the warm mud of the river, the snake suddenly lunged. Tyo dodged aside, but the creature was too quick for her and it soon had a firm grip around her body. She tried hard to get a claw-hold on the slippery skin, but to no avail. So this was the end! What a short and useless life, she thought to herself. She felt her strength slowly ebbing away as the grip tightened, and then ... grrrrrrow ... the snake went limp and Tyo rolled free into the warm water of the river.

A hot, rough tongue was licking her, and as she looked up her eyes met another pair of green eyes, larger than her own, set in an even larger black head. It was one of her own kind.

"You really shouldn't take on these things by yourself, they are much too large for you!" There was a touch of humour in his voice, as the young male jaguar spoke to her in thought language, and made gruff little comforting noises in his throat. This told Tyo that he, too, had once lived in the Old Country, although he had never actually been in Paschatland.

"Were you banished from home, too?" she asked him.

"Of course, but I left some time ago and I know this area like the back of my paw. In fact, I have it well staked out and marked. So, welcome to your new home; you are the first lady cat to visit me!"

"How did you know to come when I was in trouble?" questioned Tyo.

"Well, I heard you approaching earlier, but I was so busy trailing old Silas here," he indicated the dead anaconda, "that I was a bit late in coming to meet you. I lost him for a bit and then picked up his trail again, and look who it led me to!"

"And did you see him attack me?" Tyo seemed a little peeved that this handsome cat had actually allowed that to happen.

"Oh yes, but I had to get into just the right position to grab him. Of course, I would *never* have let him really harm you!" They rubbed noses affectionately.

Even though Tyo's mate did remember Atlantis and other places, they agreed it was best to get on with their jungle life and not talk about such things. He was a very practical cat with a thoroughly down-to-earth approach to the life he had chosen. They lived happily together for many years in what was purely an animal's world. At no time did they see any humans, although they had heard from other cats that there were some living further down the river where the jungle was less dense. And when old age finally took them back to their ancestors, Tyo was very grateful for the many lessons he had learned about the lives of the wild beasts on the Blue Planet.

Stay with old Maria and keep her company...

Life No. 4:

ITALY

After his adventures in the Amazon jungle Tyo was advised by his ancestors to take a long rest. Apparently things were not going too well on the Blue Planet and both humans and animals were having a rather hard time, so he would need to be very strong for his next adventure. Of course, Tyo had looked down on the Earth and knew the sort of thing he would have to face, but then things always tend to look a little easier when one sees them from afar. Once on top of them, however, it is a different story as many of you, no doubt, have already found out.

Tyo wanted to be with humans so that he could try to give a little happiness to someone who was very poor and unloved. "Well," he thought, "sitting here in comfort won't get the job done." So once again he closed his eyes and let himself drift off, in the way that his ancestors had taught him.

The box was hot, dusty and very dirty when Tyo opened his eyes, and he soon realized that he was a female kitten. Her mother was thin and sick, and Tyo noticed that the two other kittens who had been born to her had already returned to their ancestors. There was just Tyo and her mother. How she lived through those early days she never knew. Her poor mother had little or no milk, and had it not been for the kindly old woman who brought the occasional scrap of food she would never have survived.

One evening after Tyo had been sleeping she woke up to find her mother feeling very cold. She looked hard at her and then she knew that she, too, had returned to her ancestors. Tyo was still very young, very small and entirely alone in the world. While she was wondering what to do next, who should arrive but the old lady with a few meagre morsels for the hungry kitten. She gently turned over the cold body of Tyo's mother and then she said, in an old, gruff, but loving voice:

"Ah, *mia bambina*, now you are all alone, like old Maria. Come, stay with an old woman and keep her company in her last days."

Tyo loved the old lady, but she knew that like her mother, Maria would not be staying long in this world. Together they scavenged round the dirty back streets in the hot sun and shared what scraps of food they were able to beg or scrounge. But the old lady warned her: "Keep away from the fine people, *mia cara*, they will say you are dirty and full of disease, and will hurt you. Stay close to old Maria." Tyo did just this, but in her heart of hearts she longed to wander further afield.

Tyo had never known before what it was like to be hungry and sick, and she wondered how long she would be able to keep going in the black and white body of the little female cat in which she now lived. One day she crawled into the corner where old Maria slept, but the old lady's body was cold, just as her mother's had been, and Tyo knew that she was alone once again. Sadly she left the pile of rags in the old cellar that had been a home for Maria and herself and stepped out into the big, cruel world.

Beyond the back streets the wide roads stretched out, dusty and sunbleached. Tyo watched in wonder as the grand carriages swept past, carrying the nobles and their great ladies. She poked her head forward to get a better look, but a boot hit her in the face.

"Get off the streets, you filthy beast, bringing plague and disease to noble folk." The man who spoke wore a uniform with golden braids on it and there were big, shining buckles on his shoes.

Tyo's face hurt and her left eye wouldn't focus properly so she retreated to the darkness of a nearby alley to nurse her injury. A voice spoke in her ear.

"Miaow."

Tyo turned to face a large, black tom cat. His tail was threadbare, but he was fatter than most of her own kind that she had so far seen and his eyes were bright and friendly.

"Meow — hello," replied Tyo, and as she looked into Tom's eyes and recognized Rhe-ien, who had been her father in Atlantis, the Old Country, her little heart sang. At last she had someone who could talk to her in her own Paschat language.

"Come with me," said Tom. "These humans have no time for us. I'll show you where there's some food."

He led her through a maze of alleyways to an old storehouse. "There are fat mice and rats to be had here, girlie, and although they make you itch they're good to eat." He produced a recently slain carcass which they quickly devoured.

As the days went past Tyo and Tom mated. Because he was the biggest, strongest male in the area he was able to keep away all the other cats who would have dearly loved to have their special territory in the warehouse, with its constant supply of fresh food.

During the night Tom would take Tyo out to explore the city. It seemed that the people of these parts did not like cats very much at all. They either kicked them or threw things at them and, apart from the odd person like Maria, nobody seemed to consider that they needed to eat. On the other hand, many of the people were also hungry and sick and they quarrelled over morsels of food for their own children. So Tyo understood that with so little to eat themselves they should not wish to share it.

Tyo was expecting kittens. She could feel them inside her and counted three heartbeats. While Tom was around she would survive, but what would happen to her if something went wrong and he didn't come home one day? Tyo put the thought out of her mind and for a while life was bearable for her.

It all started one hot afternoon when Tom and Tyo were relaxing in a small patch of sunlight that had somehow managed to filter through the maze of dirty hovels in the back alley. Tom told Tyo that somebody had talked about there being a plague sweeping through the city. "We must keep well hidden," he told her. "The soldiers will come and they will burn many houses and all the things inside them and kill all animals on sight, for they blame us for the sickness."

Suddenly, there was a clatter of hooves. Soldiers on horseback appeared at the entrance to the alley and one shouted out, "Down there, Enrico, the stench is dreadful. Burn it out, or the plague will spread and reach the fine houses on the other side of the city."

Soon the lazy silence of the alley was changed to a great din. People were screaming and running in all directions, trying to salvage their few meagre belongings from their humble hovels.

"Quick," said Tom, "we must get back to the warehouse. He darted

37

across the street, but just too late. The hooves of a passing horse caught him and he was quickly trampled underfoot by the angry crowd that followed the soldiers.

Tyo crept away, full of grief. Now she was alone with her unborn kittens. She must get back to the warehouse and see if she could find some more food. It took her a long time to wend her way through the chaos back to the place that she and Tom had called home only to find, much to her horror, that it had been burned down. She heard the voices of more soldiers:

"No wonder we have plagues, a nest of disease-ridden rats. The sergent will be pleased with you, Mario, for putting an end to that filth."

As the soldiers left, Tyo crept under the charred remains of some old boxes which still held the warmth from the flames. She had to find some food for herself. Her kittens were due and they would need to be fed.

She slept on the problem for an hour or so and when she woke up she knew that there was only one thing to do; she must take a chance and go to the smart houses. After all, Tom had told her how fine nobles often left pieces of good food that were thrown into large barrels to be collected by the carters when they were full. Perhaps there might be a morsel amongst these. It was dark by then, and Tyo moved silently and slowly on her errand of life, keeping well in the shadows in case some fine person might see her and be offended by her presence. At first there was nothing and then a smell. Could it be? Yes, it was — the smell of fresh meat!

There was a pair of iron gates that seemed to lead to the back entrance of a very large house. As she was so thin, Tyo was able to squeeze through the bars easily. She followed the scent which led her across a rough courtyard to where several large, barrel-shaped objects were standing, one of which seemed to be quite warm. Tyo tried to jump to the top but it was just a little too high for her in her weakened condition. Then she noticed a sort of handle on the far side, and by using it to pull herself up she was able to look over the top and see what there was inside that smelled so good.

And there it lay, the remains of some noble person's meal, no doubt. Tyo started to tuck in for all she was worth. It was wonderful, like nothing she had ever tasted before, and fresh, too! She had eaten her fill and was just about to climb down from the bin when there was a shout.

"Hey, Marco, there's a filthy cat here, and look at the state it's in. It must surely be carrying the plague. Quick, kill it!"

Tyo tried to jump down so that she could escape, but the weight of her kittens and her own weakness prevented her from moving quickly enough. She fell to the ground and before she could regain her balance a rain of blows descended on her. For a moment the pain was dreadful, and then suddenly it was all gone.

Tyo, the Paschat, looked down and saw the two men set fire to the battered body and then he realized he was not alone. The three kittens and Rhe-ein were there, waiting for him. Tyo was happy again as the little group made their way to the places of their ancestors, to rest for a while and think about the injustices of men and the darkness that had spread over the Blue Planet.

The Cardinal loved to see kittens playing on his bed…

Life No. 5:

FRANCE

Tyo had a lot to discuss with his ancestors after his brief, sad life in Italy. He had now seen how both poor animals and humans lived and it gave him a lot to think about. It seemed very wrong to him that the rich folk had so much and the poor so little, but perhaps there was another side to the question which he felt he had to find out. Surely, there must be someone among those grand nobles who could have feelings for a little cat. So, Tyo and his ancestors agreed that he should make his next appearance on the Blue Planet at the other end of the social scale.

Tyo's new mother was long-haired, snowy white and spotlessly clean. She lived in a basket that was padded with silks and satins, and her meals were brought to her on a silver tray.

"I am a queen among cats," she told her son, for Tyo was once again a young tom, "and you are therefore a prince! Long-haired, pure white cats like us are worth a great deal of money, and soon a great noble person will choose you as his or her pet. Let us give some thought to the possibilities. Now, there is the Countess D'Orlez, or the Comte de Roquevait. Well, perhaps not him, come to think of it, as I've heard he has a bad temper, but the Duc de Boulogne is a kindly sort, and his wife is even kindlier."

As Tyo grew up his coat became longer, silkier and whiter, and Abel and Teyssadier, the two servants who looked after all the cats, would brush him regularly and comb sweet smelling herbs through his fur. Nor were Tyo and his mother the only cats around; there was Lucifer, who was very fluffy and very black; the shy Gazette; Rita, of the extra loud purr; Perruque and Racan, so named because their mother had given birth to them in the wig of the Marquis de Racan; also Pyrame, Thisbe and Soumise, who was something of a favourite.

Tyo's mother wore a silk collar with a real gold medallion hanging from it. Her own name, Mignon, was engraved on one side and on the other it said: "The property of Cardinal Armand Jean du Plessis, Duc de Richelieu."

It was a bright sunny morning when Tyo was first introduced to the Cardinal. His Eminence, for that was what he was called, had not been feeling too well and he always claimed that nothing restored his spirits more than the sight of young kittens playing on his bed. Abel placed the small bundle of white fluff on the broad counterpane and Tyo found himself looking into a pair of steely blue eyes deeply set in a lined face.

"Ah, what ecstasy!" the Cardinal exclaimed, and as he fondled the little fellow and tickled him under the chin Tyo could not help noticing the ring on his finger that had a lovely blue stone in it. Now Tyo had always loved blue stones and this one somehow reminded him of the big blue stone that the High Priest wore on a chain round his neck in the Old Country. The Cardinal had a small, pointed beard which twitched when he smiled. This made Tyo laugh and he purred loudly which seemed to please the great man. After Tyo had frolicked for a while on the big bed the Cardinal said he felt much better, and bade Abel take the little kitten back to its mother.

"That is a very fine cat," he commented. "I shall save him as a present for someone very special. We shall see."

Life with the Cardinal was both interesting and intriguing. If only a cat could write, here was history in the making. Tyo overheard conversations of great importance about other countries and their nobles, and he also learned about the "God" that people worshipped in those parts. But he was a sad and wounded God, who was hung up on two pieces of wood, and Tyo couldn't help wondering why, if people loved this God, they treated him so badly? Perhaps their God liked it that way, but Tyo didn't somehow think so.

Food at the Cardinal's palace was very good indeed and Tyo was rather upset one day when the cook scolded one of the servants for stealing the head of a trout. The poor man had apparently taken it for one of his own children! So Tyo took the head off the next fish he was given, and proudly presented it to the servant, who fled in fear at the sight! Oh dear, how could a little cat help people when they didn't speak his language?

Tyo's mother taught him how to protect their master against bad influences. She would sit on the Cardinal's lap when he was dealing with difficult or scheming people. She was able to read their thoughts and make her dislike felt in some very obvious way, like fuffing at them or growling quietly. Of course, these were all things that Tyo had learned in the Old Country, so they came very easily to him.

One day the Cardinal seemed particularly pleased for he was expecting a visit from his nephew, who was both a priest and a scholar for whom he had a great deal of affection and respect. Tyo, his mother, and three of the other cats were sitting in the Cardinal's room when the guest arrived. He was a young man with fair-hair and deep blue eyes. In fact, he reminded Tyo of someone, but at that moment the little cat wasn't quite sure who.

"Ah, Henri, we welcome you. Come, take some refreshment with us."

The two men embraced each other warmly and a servant brought in a silver tray which had tall jugs on it and a plate of lovely cakes. As the servant poured some liquid from one of the jugs into a pretty cup, the Cardinal continued:

"But why must you hide yourself away in the country when you could do so well at Court?" He pointed to a leatherbound volume that was on the table beside him. "After all, this treatise of yours is most profound and would surely win you many important friends in Paris."

The younger man answered quietly, "Uncle, I could not take the stress of life in the city. It is because I live quietly that I am able to think so clearly, and therefore write as I do."

"Oh well," said the Cardinal, "have it your own way, but the offer is open." He paused and selected a cake from the plate. "And have you thought any more of my offer to make you a Bishop? It would be a simple matter for me to make arrangements for the Diocese of Lyons, for example. You only have to say the word."

"Thank you, Uncle, but no, I am not cut out for church politics, nor do I have any wish to become caught up in Vatican intrigues. The life of a humble scholar suits me much better."

"Then how can I reward you on behalf of the church for your excellent work?" The Cardinal's eyes fell upon Tyo. "Aha, I have the very thing! Here, Henri, take this little fellow. He is a fine cat and much prized. In fact, two Duchesses I know are both hoping to receive him as a birthday gift from me, but they are frivolous females and would not appreciate the finer points of such a wise animal."

He lifted Tyo gently from the cushion on which he had been sitting and handed him to his nephew. As soon as the new hands touched him Tyo felt a familiar twinge. Could it possibly be? The younger man lifted him to his face and they both looked into each other's eyes. IT WAS! It was his own beloved Meryra from Egypt, one of the Crystal People. Tyo was so full of joy that he purred as loudly as he could as Henri cuddled him close to his heart.

"A better gift than one of God's innocent creatures you could not have made to me, Uncle. I shall cherish him for as long as I live."

The Cardinal seemed very pleased at this. After they had finished their food and drink and talked a lot more, Abel brought a fine, soft basket for Tyo, who was then taken to the apartment in the palace where Henri would be staying during his visit to Paris.

That night Henri allowed Tyo to sit on his bed and the two talked together, because they both understood thought language. Henri told Tyo many things about the world and its peoples, and about how things were run on the Blue Planet. Henri didn't think everything was as it should be either, and he wept when Tyo told him about his life in Italy. It seemed that he, too, had had a similar experience in another place and time.

A few days later they set out for the large house in the country where Henri's family lived, and where he had a whole wing to himself. Although they would often walk in the woods together Tyo seldom saw any others of his kind, but he could sometimes hear the kitchen cats mewing. On one occasion he came across a wild, striped female who lived in the barn and who, no doubt, had some beautiful, white kittens not long after their meeting.

As Tyo was so well looked after he was able to forget about the needs of his body and concentrate on learning the ways of people. Sometimes he and Henri would talk late into the night, and both of them would find it difficult to go to sleep afterwards because there were so many things that troubled them about the world and the things that went on in it. But there were happy times, too, when Tyo would sit quietly on Henri's desk while he studied the big, leather bound books in the library, or wrote down very serious things about the past and the present.

But both Tyo and Henri knew that the life of a little cat was often shorter than that of a human, so the odds were that one day Tyo would have to leave his friend. And so it was. One evening, just as the sun was setting over the lake and the trees in the far woods were nodding off to sleep, Tyo himself lay down on his dear friend's bed and quickly slipped away to join his ancestors. The quiet, gentle priest gently buried the little body under his favourite tree, and placed a large stone above it upon which was engraved: *"Mon petit Charlemagne, who was as wise as his namesake, and whom I loved more than anyone."*

And that stone still stands to this day, although you would need to search hard through the undergrowth of a certain forest in France to find it.

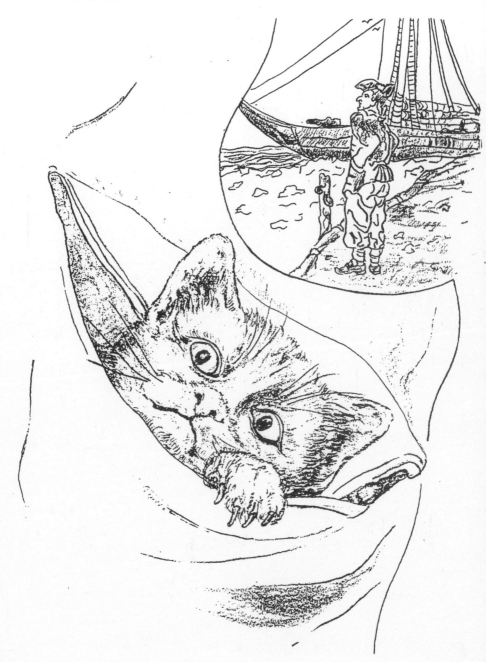

Tyo peeped out and saw many interesting things...

Life No. 6:

THE HIGH SEAS

After his good life with the Cardinal and Henri, Tyo thought that he ought to learn more about the other beings that lived on and around the Blue Planet — the fairy folk, for example. He knew that apart from very young humans and those who had inherited what they called "the sight" from their ancestors that had lived in the Old Country, there were few on Earth who were able to see and talk with fairies, or the "Spirits of the Elements," as the human sages called them. Like all other Paschats and Crystal People, Tyo, of course, could both see them and talk their language.

And so, a tom kitten was born to a plump lady cat in an old shoe box at the back of a cobbler's shop in a small port on the southwest coast of England. The cobbler was a kindly man and very fond of his black cat, whom he called Tabitha.

"Tab, me ol' darling," he would say, "'ow's about a nice piece of this juicy bacon?"

"Miaow," Tabitha would reply, for she never refused any sort of food.

"And keep an eye on that kit of yours, me darlin', 'e be alwis a-roamin' round and like as not 'e'll be pinched afore long, fine beastie that 'e is."

But Tabitha was not the most diligent of mothers. She preferred to groom herself smartly so that she could sit in the window of the little shop and be admired by the seamen who passed by. And so little Tyo wandered about inside and outside the shop as he wished, until one day his curiosity got the better of him and he decided it was time to take a look for himself at this great, big wonderful thing that everybody called "the sea."

It was only a short way to the docks. Tyo was a sturdy, well-fed, lively kitten and soon he was there, gazing in wonderment upon the beautiful waters that gave the Blue Planet its name. It was spring and the sun, which was just beginning to warm up a little, shone on Tyo's sleek black coat so that it gleamed like the gentleman's boots that the cobbler polished so brightly. The little cat was so happy that he purred with pleasure. Suddenly a rough hand closed on his neck and he was jerked up.

"See 'ere, me 'earty, yer's a fine cat, for sure. Can ye mouse? I'll wager ye can, or will when yer's a bit older. 'Tis a lucky day today for ol' Jake Morris. The Cap'n'll be right pleased when I takes ye to 'im."

Before Tyo could make so much as a squeak of protest he was whisked under the grimy coat of the seafarer who hurried back to his ship. Tyo had never been on board a ship before and as he peeped out of the old sailor's jacket he could see all sorts of interesting things. His captor took him to a cabin below deck which looked rather important, pulled him out from under his jacket, and held him up by the scruff of his neck as he boldly announced:

"There, now, Cap'n, sar. A finer looking cat I'll wager ye'll never find in these parts — an' a tom, too!"

The Captain, a huge figure of a man with a thick brown beard, of which he was obviously very proud, puffed at his pipe and eyed Tyo carefully. Now, because Tyo was pure black, which sailors considered a sign of good luck, the Captain welcomed his presence on board.

"Aye, 'tis a good animal, Jake. Ye'v done well. Put 'im in the 'old and let 'im out to sniff round a bit after we casts off. And mind 'e's fed and watered; a sick cat ain't no good to any ship." As an afterthought he added: "An' as 'e be black as coal, we'll call 'im Sooty!"

"Aye, aye, Cap'n," smiled Jake, as he gathered Tyo up and carried him down to the ship's fo'c'sle, where it was very dark and a bit damp.

"See 'ere, feller, ol' Jake'll find ye a nice blanket, as befits a pretty creature as yer, and a drop of gravy, too, mebbe." He was away for a few minutes, but soon returned with the remnants of what had been an old brown rug, and a cracked bowl which contained some cold broth. "Many's the tale ol' Jake'll tell ye after we sets sail. This ship's called the Katy

Jane. The ol' man named 'er after one of 'is fancy ladies in the colonies," old Jake explained to Tyo, "and a stout ship she be, too — like 'er namesake, I'll wager," he chuckled heartily.

It was not long before the ship put to sea, after which Tyo was allowed to roam wherever he wanted except when there was a storm, but that was only to prevent him from being swept away by the big waves. The Katy Jane's cargo was mainly grain and spices, so a good mouser, which Tyo indeed turned out to be, was a great help to the Captain and his crew, for there were always fat mice and rats to catch in the hold. The sailors were rough but kind, for black cats were considered good luck.

Ships in those days did not have refrigerators so there was not much variety in the diet except when they put into port. Fresh water also became scarce after they had been at sea for some time, but the Captain was a good seaman and always managed to get his ship into port before everything ran out. But a few times old Jake and the other sailors had to share their portions of salt beef with Tyo when rations were short and the mice were hard to find.

As time went by Tyo also became very friendly with the First Mate, a huge, red-haired, freckled-faced man named Mallory. That was his only name, or at least the only name he had that anybody knew about. Mallory was not averse to a good fight and often picked one with one of the other men, "Just to keep me muscles in trim," he would say.

Mallory liked to use the time when he was off watch to fish from the ship's stern, and whatever he caught he shared with Tyo. Just like Jake, Mallory also liked to talk to Tyo. In fact, Tyo had never come across so many big, rough-looking men who were happy to spend long periods talking to a big, black tom cat. Mallory would tell Tyo tales of former voyages, of sea monsters, and of the spirits of long-dead seamen who walked the waters at certain places on the high seas. He also boasted that his family had been seafaring folk for generations back to the time of Sir Francis Drake himself! Although Tyo believed some of these stories, others he knew were fantasies, but it didn't really matter because it made Mallory happy to talk about them. Tyo would sit quietly and when he cocked his ears attentively Mallory would say:

"Ye see, Sooty, me boy, yers is clever, yers is! Yers knows a lot and yers listens, and that's what I likes about ye. 'Ave a nice bit of grub for yer's trouble." And so saying he would toss Tyo a tasty morsel, "'Ere's a 'erring 'ead for ye, because yer's is a good cat!"

Jake also told many strange stories, some tall and some not so tall. Tyo learned that he had once been married and had a pretty wife called May, and a beautiful little daughter with long, dark curls, whose name was Peggy. But while he had been away at sea some soldiers had marched in and taken them prisoner, and all because May had been accused of being a witch because she had made a herbal potion for a sick neighbour, which was supposed to have offended their "God". But because the prison had been such a dreadful place, both of them had died before May's name was cleared. Tyo could not help wondering what kind of "God" would let innocent women and little children die like that, for no reason. He was very glad that he was a Paschat and knew about the Old Ones, who were always just, kind, loving and caring. Because of his sad loss, Jake no longer wished to be on the land where such bad people lived and preferred to stay at sea as much as he could.

"The sea's a right strange place, alright," he would say, "an' a stranger place ye'll never find, I'll be bound. An' 'tain't all bad things that ye 'ears on deck on a dark night. I've 'eard ladies a-singin', only it weren't human-like ladies. An' I've 'eard me little girlie a-callin' to me an' a-sayin': 'Daddy, don't yer fret, now — I'm with them pretty ladies what sings.' I reckon as 'ow she means them sea-nymphs what sings at night, and not them angels they talks about in church."

Of course, Tyo knew what they were, but he couldn't tell Jake. On a calm night Tyo would sit on the deck by himself and talk to the Water Ondines, and they would bring him messages from the distant stars that the Paschats and Crystal People had visited during their space travels. The Ondines would sing their songs for him, and from those songs he learned all about the ways of Water on the Blue Planet, as well as the ways of the other three elements: Fire, Air and Earth.

The Katy Jane visited many foreign parts during her travels and Tyo was not usually allowed to go ashore. However, on one occasion he did manage to hide among the sacks of cargo that were being unloaded and found himself in a most mysterious place. Humans of many different races were milling about and making a lot of noise. There were some black people who were all chained together and being driven along by brown people with cloths wound around their heads, and who hit them with whips until they cried out in pain. Tyo recalled seeing this also during his days in Egypt where they were called "captives". Here they were slaves being traded and sold for profit, and he was sad in his little heart for all those who suffered on the Blue Planet.

Since no-one seemed to notice him, Tyo stole silently around the back of some large boxes which looked interesting. He failed, however, to see the dark figure of a man who was taking a short rest on one of them. As he was having a suspicious sniff around, a hand suddenly caught him by the tail and swung him aloft.

"What have we here? A fat cat, I do declare! A fine meal he'll make for a hungry family," the thin, dark-skinned man said as he eyed Tyo.

Now, Tyo had never been picked up by the tail before and it hurt him so much that his little body twisted around violently with the pain. The movement, however, brought him near enough to the man's arm to get a good claw hold.

"Ooowwwwwww," the man cried out, hastily dropping his little prize. Tyo withdrew his claws, dropped to the ground and ran off as fast as his four legs would carry him to hide among the packing cases. Once back in the safety of the ship he resolved he would never go ashore again, unless it was with one of his trusty sailor friends.

Tyo sailed on many voyages with the Katy Jane and her crew. Sometimes a man would leave and another take his place, but always there was this strong bond between the men and their lucky black cat. Before they went ashore they would often come and touch him on the head. "Bring us some luck, now, won't ye, Soot," they would say. And sure enough, something pleasant would happen for them that day.

As the years passed and he grew older Tyo's eyes started to grow dim, but the Captain would not part with him. "Ol' Sooty's brought good luck to this ship and them that's sailed on 'er under my command these many years," he would say to his men. 'Taint right to get rid of 'im jist 'cause 'e's gettin' old, and throw good luck away like that!" And there wasn't a man among them who didn't agree with the Captain.

Secretly, of course, the men's feelings for Tyo were far deeper and more personal than they let on to each other. Being big, rough and tough sailors, it did not do to let anyone know how they really felt, but the little black cat had become like one of their family, and Tyo knew it.

One dark night on the high seas there was a terrible storm. Winds blew to gale force and the crew were hard pressed to keep the old vessel afloat. Of course, Tyo knew about the impending storm well before it happened, as he had been forewarned by the Water Ondines and the Sylphs of the Air, who blew up the storms in the first place. As the ship rocked and shuddered on the huge waves, a strong gust of wind broke off part of the main mast, which hit Mallory as it fell and wounded him badly. Gradually the storm seemed to ease off, but they were miles from the nearest port and there was no doctor on board to save the First Mate's life. As he lay in his hammock dying, he asked Jake to bring Tyo to him.

"Lay ol' Sooty next to me, Jake, close by me 'eart." Jake placed Tyo beside Mallory and Tyo pressed lovingly against the huge frame.

"I'm on me way out, ol' friend." His voice grew weaker and he faltered, his next words being barely a whisper. "Seeing as 'ow thee and me 'ave been shipmates these past years — and thee's old, too — when I'm gone over I'll wait for ye, Soot. Yer's all I've ever had, so don't yer be long..."

And with those words Mallory left to join his ancestors. His mates buried him at sea, while the old Captain said nice things about him and read from a little black book. But from that moment on Tyo knew no peace of mind. Now completely blind, he would pace the deck and hear Mallory's voice saying, "I'll wait for ye, Soot!"

And one day Tyo knew it was time. It was a warm, calm spring morning when Tyo lay down on some old sacks in the fo'c'sle and kept his appointment with his friend. And, sure enough, there was Mallory waiting for him, arms outstretched. Only it wasn't the red-haired giant seaman that he had known; it was his sister Taku who met him, and together they made their way back to the place of their ancestors.

Old Jake wrapped the body of the small black cat as tenderly as if it had been his own daughter, and as he dropped it gently over the side he whispered: "Go ye to my dear May an' sweet Peggy, an' to the sea-ladies what sings at night, and wait ye there 'till yer ol' shipmate Jake joins yer."

They both retreated until each had disappeared...

Life No. 7:

.

INDIA

Although life aboard the Katy Jane had been rough at times, Tyo had been happy with the kindly seamen who had taught him a great deal about the ways of humans. But conditions on the Blue Planet were changing fast. Wars had been fought, empires lost and won, and there were new values among people that could well affect the lives of animals, particularly wild ones. Tyo knew that there were some branches of the cat family that could be very cruel and unkind, so he felt he should spend some time in their company and try to understand what made them behave that way.

He became aware once again of the world, as the broad, rough tongue of his brightly striped mother cleared away the scales of birth. He sniffed the air, which was warm and moist and certainly smelled differently from anything he had known before. There was no brother or sister tiger to keep him company and, although his mother was very strong, she was also very nervous. He tried to ask her what was the matter, but she just licked him tenderly and told him not to worry his little head about such things until he was old enough to understand them. As he grew larger and stronger she taught him to hunt for food and, what was just as important, to protect himself. For unlike his life as a jaguar in the Amazon, where the only enemies were other animals, this time Tyo would have to face a far more fearsome foe — man!

It was not long before Tyo met other tigers who told him how humans came in parties to hunt them, kill as many as they could find and take away their skins to be made into rugs, or hung on the walls of their houses. There was one crotchety old male who would sit in his lair and tell gory stories about the great beasts he had seen killed by the loud fire sticks, and their coats stolen. The old chap was not the most pleasant of characters himself, mind you, as he also told tales of the people he had occasionally killed and eaten, so perhaps he had given these men some cause to hunt the great striped cats.

Tyo's mother had insisted that he go out on his own as soon as he was strong enough to feed and defend himself, and for a while he roamed the dense undergrowth with two other young males who were in the same situation. But soon their competition for territory grew strong. Never being much of a fighter, Tyo decided to leave the other two to sort it out between themselves while he travelled further afield in search of a mate. For many weeks he prowled cautiously through the dense jungle undergrowth, always taking care to move on if he found the markings of other male beasts. And then, one very wet morning, he discovered the perfect area to stake out as his own. By this time he was a very large and very strong tiger; just the kind, in fact, that humans took pride in shooting.

The rains seemed to last forever, but by the time they stopped Tyo had marked his territory well and was ready to invite a tigress to share it with him. The damp undergrowth steamed under the hot sun as Tyo set out one bright morning on his new quest.

Now it is the custom for male tigers to give a special kind of call when they are looking for a female, so Tyo patrolled his patch and did just this. But unknown to him there was a hunting party in the area that day and his call attracted their attention.

Tyo stood quite still in the high, matted foliage, hoping that no one would see him, but the beaters were now heading in his direction and getting closer and closer. He could hear the babble of their voices and detect the scent of elephants in the distance, and he was very frightened.

Perhaps he would have to stand and defend himself, but he had no taste for killing humans even in self-defence. Suddenly there was a roar, followed instantly by the crack of a gun, and through a small break in the tangled growth Tyo saw another yellow and black body slumped on the ground before the hunting party in the clearing ahead.

"Got him? Why, it's a female, you fool, I thought you said you heard a male out there!"

"That was the call of a male tiger, *sahib*, of that I am very sure."

"Rubbish, boy, they all sound the same to me."

As Tyo peeped cautiously between the tall blades of grass he could see some of the humans quite clearly. There was a big, red-faced man with a fat belly and a handlebar moustache who was dressed in some sort of uniform, while the younger man he was talking to was slim, brown-skinned and simply clad in a tattered cloth knotted around his waist.

"There could be another out there, *sahib*. That was a male mating call, I am thinking."

"And I am thinking not!" the older man bellowed, as he beckoned to another man in uniform who was standing nearby and holding a rifle. "Come on, Hawkins, two's enough for one morning. See that this lot is organized and let's get out of here; I could use a cold, stiff drink!"

As he turned away he spoke again to the native. "If you think there's another tiger out there, boy, why don't you just call 'pussy, pussy, pussy' and the bloody beast might come, what!"

He roared with laughter as he strode away and Tyo heard him say to the other officer, "These bloody natives think they know animal language, superstitious nonsense..." The rest of the conversation was lost in the mists of the forest.

The brown-skinned young man stood alone for a moment and a look of anger and defiance crossed his face. Slowly and deliberately, with rifle at the ready, he started to walk towards the undergrowth where Tyo was hiding and the young tiger knew that if he came any closer he would see him and shoot. Tyo tried to edge silently back into the safety of the jungle, but the human also moved steadily forward, coming nearer with each step. Then suddenly Tyo trod on a fallen branch which broke with a loud snap. Using the barrel of his rifle the man cautiously parted the tall undergrowth behind which Tyo was hiding.

For a moment they stood and faced each other — man and tiger — and Tyo realized this was not the first time they had met. Long ago in the Old Country there had been a young priest called Indris who had been brought to the great Temple for judgment, accused of a crime of which he was not guilty. It had been Tyo's first judgment and as a little lioness she had seen innocence in his aura. Of course, Tyo remembered it all quite clearly and he wondered whether the young man who faced him did also.

They looked deeply into each other's eyes and for a moment neither one moved. It was Tyo who first started to back slowly away, and as he did so the young man slowly lowered his gun and also took a step backwards. And so they both retreated until each had disappeared completely from the other's view.

From a distance Tyo heard the older man shout, "Well, boy, find your pussy-cat, eh?"

"No, *sahib*," was the reply. "I am sorry, *sahib*, I must have been mistaken. There was nothing there at all."

"I should think not, either. You can't fool me, boy, I've been in this game too long," he said dismissively.

"Yes, *sahib*, you are indeed right," the young native boy said, and with that the men departed.

Tyo did find a mate and together they managed to survive for several years and raise many cubs. But eventually, he, too, was tracked down and shot by men riding on the back of an elephant, and for many years his fine pelt could be seen adorning the walls of a large country house in England.

Tyo, the Paschat, returned once more to the place of his ancestors and pondered the cruelty and inhumanity of the human race.

Tatiana clutched 'Triska' close to her heart...

Life No. 8:

RUSSIA

Although Tyo had once sacrificed his life to save Meryra, but that had been for someone he truly loved. Could he also make the same sacrifice for a stranger, he asked himself? He had heard of humans who had done this, so why not a Paschat?

The night was dark, and a chill wind was chasing the first snow flurries of winter across the grey streets of St. Petersburg. Inside the tall house all was quiet and a roaring fire blazed in the huge fireplace as little Tatiana's pet cat gave birth to two blue-grey kittens, one male and one female, in the softly lined basket.

"Come quickly, Anna Ivanova, Mishkin has had her babies!" Tatiana called excitedly.

Her elderly nanny waddled into the room as fast as her short legs would carry her.

"Let old Anna have a look, my little snowflake," for that was her special name for the little girl she had cared for and been a constant companion to since she was a tiny baby. The nanny peered hard into the little mass of wet fur, but was greeted with some appropriate growls and hisses from Mishkin. "Let the little mother be alone with her kittens for a while, my darling. She will let us know when we may look at them. They are alive and well, and that is what matters now."

61

Tatiana Ilytsianova was just ten years old. Her parents already had three grown up sons when she was born, each of whom had followed their father's footsteps into the Army. She was therefore a lonely child, which was why Mishkin meant so much to her. Of course, Tyo was one of Mishkin's kittens. He was now a little female who Tatiana named Triska, while her brother, Boris, eventually became known as Bobo the Fearless — a title which surely speaks for itself!

The kittens thrived, but one day Tatiana's parents had Mishkin taken away to have an operation so that she would not have any more kittens. She never came back, and when Anna told Tatiana that she had died during the operation the little girl was heartbroken. From that moment on, Tatiana transferred all her affection to Triska and a deep bond developed between them. In time, Triska and Bobo were also taken away for surgery, and fortunately both survived. Tyo really liked being a Russian Blue, since he had never been one before, and as Triska grew older and stronger her coat became more and more beautiful.

But, as Tyo had already learned through several lives, things seldom run smoothly for very long where humans are concerned. One day when Tatiana returned home in the carriage, after visiting the house of her parents' friends, she suddenly burst into tears and cried long and hard on Tyo's back. "What shall we do, little Triska, if they drive us away, too?"

Tyo was not quite sure what it was all about, although he was able to read enough of Tatiana's thoughts to know that she and her family were in some kind of danger.

Anna comforted her: "Dry your tears, little snowflake. Old Anna will take care you."

"And I know you will, dear Anna Ivanova. But do be careful what you say to the coachman, Yuri Mikhailovich. I do not trust the man and feel he is an enemy!"

"Come, come now, my darling, has he not been in service here for twenty years or more? Why would he betray us?" Like Tatiana, Tyo also suspected that all was not well among the household staff, but neither of them could tell Anna, for she would not understand.

It was not long before the situation became worse. There had been riots in the streets for some time and Tyo had become used to the noise and clatter. But on this night it was different. The heavily bolted doors and windows of the mansion were being smashed in and the mob was trying to enter. Tatiana's brothers had arrived on the scene some days earlier and had begun preparations for a hasty departure. So, when her brother Alexei instructed the servants to take them to safety, Anna had a warm cloak ready and some clothes packed for Tatiana, and a cosy basket for Triska and Bobo.

But things did not work out quite as planned. They managed to escape from the house through a secret cellar and make their way to the outskirts of the city, but they were discovered by a band of army deserters who, when seeing Alexei in his uniform, set upon him. Although they fought bravely, Alexei and the servants were killed by the mob, but the grieving and frightened Tatiana and Anna managed to escape in the confusion and hide among the shattered buildings until the noise and confusion had died down.

For a while they wandered in the countryside together, not knowing where to go, until they finally met up with other refugees like themselves who had managed to escape the anger of the revolutionary crowd. After much discussion, the little group decided to make their way to the woods in the north and try to get to Russia's border with Finland, as the people of those parts were kindly disposed towards helping refugees. But the weather was bitterly cold and the going was hard. The travellers, mainly women and children, with two elderly male retainers, were soon exhausted and the younger children were crying with cold and hunger.

The thick forest protected them from the revolutionaries, but there was little food to be had and matters were becoming desperate. Of course, the cats had not been fed either, although Tatiana let them out now and again to catch little creatures of the night. It was Bobo the Fearless, in pursuit of a ground squirrel, who brought the attention of the travellers to the fact that he was faring better than they were. As he darted in front of a young, dark-haired lady trying to comfort her shivering child, the woman cried out, "Catch that cat and kill it, Nicolai, and we will have some supper tonight."

No sooner had the woman spoken when one of the men grabbed Bobo by the scruff of the neck, while the woman made haste to prepare his body for the fire. Of course, Tatiana could not eat the morsels of food that were passed around the warm fire that evening. Her own hunger grew, but her fear that someone might discover Triska became even greater. Terrified of losing her only surviving love, she silently withdrew deeper into the forest, clutching the basket containing Triska close to her heart.

And so another day passed as the cold and starving party trudged wearily onward. Two babies had died during the night of the cold and lack of milk. Only three children now remained although they, too, were beginning to fail. Now, Tyo knew intuitively that one more day would see them safely in the village that lay ahead, where the friendly townspeople would welcome and feed them. But could the children make it? There was only one way — a sacrifice had to be made. Tatiana and Anna had made sure to keep well away from the others when they let Triska out of her basket to forage for food and take care of the call of nature. But this time, as darkness fell and the basket lid was opened, Triska ran straight toward the little group of cold, starving people and offered herself.

A woman's voice cried out, "Look, there's another cat! Get it quickly, Igor. My prayer to the Ikon has been answered."

Rough hands closed around Triska's neck and in a moment it was all over. But as Tyo, the Paschat, paused happily over the figures of the hungry children as they ate, he became aware of another figure standing by his side. It was dear Meryra. Below, in the dark depth of the forest, an old woman stood weeping over the body of a little girl who had died clutching a small basket to her broken heart.

Tyo and Meryra returned together to their ancestors, each knowing that the sacrifice had been worth it.

Tyo recognised the Sekhmet figure immediately...

Life No. 9:

WALES

Tyo knew that he was coming to the end of the time that the Old Ones had granted him to study the ways of all life forms, and help as much as he could on the Blue Planet. After conferring with his ancestors, and while he was thinking seriously about what he had to do next, he heard the voice of Taku calling to him: "Tyo, come to us, we are all here together now; please come, please!"

Tyo answered, "Of course, I'll come, but where? And how do I get there?"

"Follow the sound of our voices and think 'Somali'," Taku replied.

So Tyo listened carefully to the voices and thought Somali as hard as he could, and as he did he knew he was being drawn to his next mother. When he first opened his golden eyes Tyo found himself looking into a pair of soft brown ones that belonged to a middle-aged lady.

"Welcome, little mancat," she whispered gently to him. "We were expecting you, for you were promised to my niece before you were born. However, you must stay here with your nice, brown mother until you are old enough to leave."

Tyo was once again an only kitten, and as he cuddled close to his new mother's tawny coloured tummy something told him that this mother could talk in the same way that he could. He sent out a thought to her and she was quick to reply.

"Yes, little one, I was in the Old Country also, and I know all about Paschats like yourself. Soon you will leave me and go to a place where others of your kind will be waiting for you, and where you will help them in the same way that you did in the Old Country."

"Where shall I go, Mother?" Tyo asked.

"Not far from here someone is waiting for you, so grow strong and beautiful. You will need all your strength for your tasks ahead, since this is the last time you and your Paschat kin will be here on the Blue Planet," she replied.

And so Tyo stayed with his beautiful mother, whose magnificent plume of a tail waved daintily among the spring flowers in the well-tended garden. Tyo also grew to be beautiful and strong, with eyes like his mother's, but his coat was like his father's — a rich sorrel colour which gleamed in the bright sunlight.

One day visitors arrived; a man and a lady, who came in a big, shiny car. Tyo caught a glimpse of the man, but did not recognize him. Well, not at first anyway, but he knew it wasn't Taku. And then he saw the lady. She had reddish hair and freckles, and her eyes were a soft grey. Around her neck she wore a golden chain on the end of which dangled something that Tyo recognized immediately — a little gold Sekhmet figure, just like the Paschat statues in the old Egyptian temples. He was so excited that he jumped off the table onto the lady's shoulder, leaned over and cuffed the dangling ornament, as the lady stroked him lovingly.

"There, there, you can play with this as much as you like," she said, removing it from her neck. But Tyo no longer wanted the pendant, for in the lady's touch and the sound of her voice he recognized his own dear sister, Taku!

She took him gently down from her shoulder and cuddled him closely, while Tyo nuzzled up and tried to show her that he knew who she was. The man spoke:

"You see, my dear, he recognizes you, just as we were told. What will you call him?"

There was a pause while the lady gently rubbed Tyo's plump tummy. "Why, Tyo, of course, what else!" They laughed merrily together and soon they were off in the shiny car to Tyo's new home.

Keridwen and Dylan, for that was what the man and woman were called, had an eight year-old daughter named Merlin. You can imagine Tyo's surprise when he recognized her as the kindly Meryra he had known in Egypt, and who had also been with him in other lives. And it did not take him long either to realize that Dylan was his old shipmate, Jake, who had at last found the loved ones he lost all those years ago.

But that was not all. There were also two other cats — an old brown Burmese named Arthur, and a little female tabby who had come to them as a stray, whom they named Rhiannon. Now do I need to tell you that they were Rhe-ien and Shana?

And so Tyo, his Paschat family, and their Crystal friends are here in today's world, working hard for the rights of animals, the conservation of the land for the fairy people, the protection of the trees they loved so dearly on their own planet, and the healing of all living things that might need their help.

Now, for all you know, you might have Paschats and Crystal People as your next door neighbours, because Keridwen, Dylan and Merlin are not their real names, of course. But I couldn't tell you them, now could I?